INTRODUCTION

Welcome to The Lad's Air-Frying Bible – the only cookbook you'll ever need if you've got an appetite, a bit of common sense, and an air fryer that's not just gathering dust next to your toaster.

This book isn't about fancy micro herbs or spending half your night peeling things. It's for lads like us – hungry, a bit skint sometimes, and after food that actually tastes like something. Whether you're cooking for yourself, trying to impress someone, or just fed up of eating beige sadness out the microwave – you're in the right place.

I've packed these pages with meals that are cheap, easy, and proper tasty. Some are spicy, some are stodgy, and some are just downright filthy (in the best way). All of them are doable. No need for posh gear or a culinary diploma – just chuck it in, set the timer, and let the air fryer work its magic.

By the end of this book, you'll know how to knock up legendary breakfasts, quick dinners, and those late-night "need something now" fixes. You'll learn a few tricks along the way – like how to make wings that slap, chips that actually crunch, and the kind of traybakes that fill your freezer and your belly.

So fire up the beast, mate. It's time to learn how to cook like a legend.

The Lad's Air-Frying Bible

Simple. Cheap. Tasty as hell.

INTRO

Why the Air Fryer is Your New Wingman Gear, Grub & Getting Started
No-Nonsense Ingredients List

WHY THE AIR FRYER IS YOUR NEW WINGMAN

Let's get this straight – the air fryer isn't just a kitchen gadget. It's your ride-or-die. Your secret weapon. Your crispy little life-saver when you're skint, starving, or just can't be bothered to wash a pan.

Why's it such a game-changer? Because it cooks fast, it's cheaper to run than your oven, and it doesn't need constant babysitting. You whack stuff in, press a button, and ten minutes later you've got something golden, crunchy, and mouth-watering. Magic, basically.

And it's not just for chips, mate. You can do everything from wings and burgers to brownies and full-on roast dinners if you know what you're doing. Which you're about to.

Plus, there's barely any mess. Most of the time, it's just one tray to clean. That means less washing up and more time eating, chilling, or doing absolutely nowt.

So if your idea of cooking is usually a pot noodle and a prayer – this book's going to change your life.

GEAR, GRUB & GETTING STARTED

Right – before we start chucking chicken in and hoping for the best, let's get you sorted with the basics.

The Gear

You need an air fryer. Not a spaceship. Just one that works. Digital or manual, basket or dual-drawer – don't stress. If it gets hot and has a timer, it'll do the job. If yours looks like it came from the back of a car boot sale, no shame. We're here to cook, not flex.

Optional extras? Tongs. Foil. Maybe a little silicone liner if you're proper lazy with washing up. That's it.

The Grub

This book sticks to everyday ingredients. We're talking supermarket basics, nothing wild. Chicken, sausages, frozen chips, cheese, wraps, pasta, a few spices. Stuff you've probably already got in your kitchen... or can grab from Lidl without taking out a loan.

Stock up on some seasoning: smoked paprika, garlic powder, chilli flakes, and salt and pepper. With those, you can make anything taste like a tenner meal for under a fiver.

Getting Started

Always preheat your air fryer unless it says not to. Five minutes at 180°C usually does the trick. Give the tray a little spray of oil if you're cooking stuff that might stick. Not too much – this isn't deep frying, it's air-frying. Healthier, cleaner, and still bangin'.

And one last tip before we dive in: don't be scared to experiment. The best meals come from having a go. Mess it up? Try again. Burn it? That's character.

You ready? Let's cook.

INSIDE AN AIR FRYER

HEATING
ELEMENT

CHAPTER ONE
WAKE UP & EAT

HOT AIR
BLAST

1.BACON & EGG CRUMPET STACKS
2.CHORIZO BREAKFAST HASH
3.SAUSAGE & BEAN TOASTIE BOMBS

CRISPER
BASKET

BACON & EGG CRUMPET STACKS

This one's filthy in the best way. Soft buttery crumpets, crispy bacon, gooey fried egg, and a dash of hot sauce or ketchup if you're feeling bold. Forget McMuffins – this is the king of breakfast stacks.

You'll need:

3 crumpets

2 rashers of smoked back bacon

2 eggs

A knob of butter

Salt, pepper, and whatever sauce makes you smile

Method:

Preheat your air fryer to 200°C.

Lay the bacon flat in the basket and cook for 8-10 minutes, flipping halfway. You want it crispy but still juicy.

While that's cooking, toast your crumpets – either in the toaster or in the air fryer for 2-3 minutes.

Crack the eggs into silicone muffin moulds or a small foil dish. Air fry at 180°C for about 6 minutes until the whites are set and yolk's still soft.

Stack it up: crumpet, bacon, egg. Repeat if you're extra hungry. Add butter and sauce. Smash it.

Lad Tip: Want to make it even filthier? Add a slice of cheese between layers and let it melt. Game over.

CHORIZO BREAKFAST HASH

Spicy, smoky, crunchy, and satisfying as hell. This hash is your new go-to when you wake up starving and don't want to wait an hour for a fry-up. Packed with flavour, dead easy, and you'll want seconds before you've finished the first.

You'll need:
1 large potato (or a handful of frozen hash browns if you're cheating – no judgement)
100g chorizo, sliced or cubed
Half a red onion, chopped
1 egg
Smoked paprika, salt, and pepper
Bit of oil spray
Method:

If using a raw potato, chop it small – think dice-sized chunks – and air fry at 200°C with a spray of oil and a pinch of salt and paprika. Give it 15–18 minutes, shake halfway.
Chuck in the onion and chorizo for the last 7 minutes so it all crisps up and the chorizo oils coat the spuds.

Crack an egg right on top and air fry at 180°C for 5–6 minutes until the white sets and the yolk stays runny.
Slide it onto a plate and let the yolk ooze through the crispy, spicy goodness.

Lad Tip: Got some leftover peppers or mushrooms in the fridge? Chuck 'em in. This hash don't judge.

SAUSAGE & BEAN TOASTIE BOMBS

This one's a full English wrapped in a pocket of crispy, golden joy. Baked beans, sausage, and cheese stuffed inside bread, sealed, and air-fried until it crunches when you bite. No crumbs left behind.

You'll need:
2 slices of white bread (the squidgy kind works best)
2 cooked sausages (Cumberland, Lincolnshire, or whatever's in the fridge)
2 tbsp baked beans
Handful of grated cheddar
Bit of butter or oil spray
Method:
Preheat the air fryer to 190°C.
Flatten your bread slices with a rolling pin or glass – we want them thin enough to seal.
Chop up the sausages and mix with beans and cheese. Keep it chunky but not leaking.
Spoon the mix into the centre of the bread, then fold it over like a pasty. Press the edges down hard with a fork to seal.
Spray or butter the outside lightly, then into the air fryer for 6-8 minutes until golden, crispy, and oozing cheese.

Lad Tip: Want heat? Add a bit of hot sauce or chopped jalapeños to the mix.
Boom.

BANG BANG CHICKEN BITES

STICKY, SPICY, AND DANGEROUSLY ADDICTIVE. THESE LITTLE BEAUTIES ARE CRISPY CHICKEN CHUNKS TOSSED IN A CREAMY, FIERY SAUCE THAT HITS SWEET, SALTY, AND SPICY ALL AT ONCE. YOU'LL BE LICKING YOUR FINGERS AND LOOKING FOR MORE BEFORE THEY'VE EVEN COOLED DOWN.

YOU'LL NEED:
2 CHICKEN BREASTS, CHOPPED INTO BITE-SIZED PIECES
2 TBSP CORNFLOUR
SALT, PEPPER, GARLIC POWDER
OIL SPRAY
FOR THE SAUCE:
3 TBSP MAYO
2 TBSP SWEET CHILLI SAUCE
1 TBSP SRIRACHA (MORE IF YOU'RE FEELING BRAVE)
1 TSP HONEY
METHOD:
TOSS THE CHICKEN PIECES IN CORNFLOUR, SALT, PEPPER, AND GARLIC POWDER TILL COATED.
PREHEAT THE AIR FRYER TO 200°C.
LAY THE CHICKEN OUT IN A SINGLE LAYER, SPRAY WITH OIL, AND COOK FOR 12–15 MINUTES – SHAKE HALFWAY UNTIL THEY'RE GOLDEN AND CRISP.
WHILE THAT'S FRYING, MIX UP YOUR SAUCE IN A BOWL. TASTE IT. ADJUST FIRE LEVELS TO YOUR LIKING.
WHEN THE CHICKEN'S DONE, TOSS IT IN THE SAUCE WHILE IT'S HOT SO IT STICKS AND SOAKS IN THE FLAVOUR.
SERVE IT UP WITH A SIDE OF FRIES, RICE, OR JUST EAT IT WITH YOUR HANDS LIKE AN ANIMAL. YOU'VE EARNED IT.

LAD TIP: WANT TO TURN THIS INTO A BANGING WRAP? STUFF THE CHICKEN INTO A TORTILLA WITH LETTUCE AND A HANDFUL OF CRUSHED NACHOS. TRUST ME.

INSIDE AN AIR FRYER

HEATING
ELEMENT

CHAPTER TWO:
THE SPICE SECTION

HOT AIR
BLASTER

CRISPER
BASKET

JAMAICAN JERK WINGS

THESE BAD BOYS ARE SPICY, SMOKY, AND STRAIGHT-UP ADDICTIVE. PROPER JERK FLAVOUR WITHOUT STANDING OVER A BBQ FOR THREE HOURS. YOU'LL FEEL LIKE A KING IN YOUR OWN KITCHEN – AND YOUR MATES WILL THINK YOU'RE A GENIUS.

YOU'LL NEED:
8-10 CHICKEN WINGS (OR DRUMSTICKS IF THAT'S WHAT YOU'VE GOT)
1 TBSP JERK SEASONING (WET PASTE IS BEST, BUT DRY RUB WORKS TOO)
1 TBSP OIL
JUICE OF HALF A LIME
1 TSP HONEY
PINCH OF SALT
METHOD:
IN A BOWL, TOSS THE WINGS WITH JERK SEASONING, OIL, LIME JUICE, HONEY, AND A BIT OF SALT. COAT EVERY BIT – NO WING LEFT BEHIND.
LET THEM SIT FOR 10-15 MINS IF YOU'VE GOT TIME, OR OVERNIGHT IF YOU'RE PLANNING AHEAD (BUT WHO DOES THAT?)
PREHEAT THE AIR FRYER TO 200°C.
COOK THE WINGS FOR 20-25 MINUTES, TURNING ONCE OR TWICE SO THEY GET CRISPY ON ALL SIDES AND SLIGHTLY CHARRED.
SERVE WITH LIME WEDGES, COLD DRINK, AND MAYBE A FAN IF YOU'VE OVERDONE THE HEAT.

LAD TIP: GOT A SWEET TOOTH? ADD A SPLASH OF MANGO CHUTNEY TO THE MARINADE FOR A SPICY-SWEET KICK. SOUNDS WRONG. TASTES RIGHT.

HOT HONEY HALLOUMI

THIS IS THE KIND OF SIDE DISH THAT STEALS THE WHOLE MEAL. GOLDEN HALLOUMI BITES WITH A SPICY HONEY DRIZZLE – CRUNCHY OUTSIDE, SOFT IN THE MIDDLE, AND SO MOREISH YOU'LL BE GUARDING THE PLATE LIKE A DRAGON.

YOU'LL NEED:
1 BLOCK OF HALLOUMI, CHOPPED INTO CHUNKY BITES
1 TBSP CORNFLOUR
PINCH OF SMOKED PAPRIKA
BIT OF OIL SPRAY
FOR THE HOT HONEY:
2 TBSP HONEY
1 TSP CHILLI FLAKES (MORE IF YOU'RE A MENACE)
1 TSP HOT SAUCE (OPTIONAL BUT ELITE)
METHOD:
PAT THE HALLOUMI DRY SO IT CRISPS UP. TOSS THE CHUNKS IN CORNFLOUR AND PAPRIKA.
PREHEAT THE AIR FRYER TO 200°C.
SPRAY THE BASKET AND LAY THE HALLOUMI OUT IN A SINGLE LAYER. COOK FOR 8-10 MINUTES, FLIPPING HALFWAY, UNTIL GOLDEN AND CRISPY.
WHILE THEY'RE COOKING, WARM THE HONEY SLIGHTLY (MICROWAVE OR HOB), STIR IN CHILLI FLAKES AND HOT SAUCE.
WHEN THE HALLOUMI'S DONE, DRIZZLE THAT HOT HONEY STRAIGHT OVER THE TOP WHILE IT'S STILL SIZZLING. SERVE FAST – THEY DON'T HANG AROUND.

LAD TIP: PAIR IT WITH A SIDE OF CHILLI JAM OR USE IT TO UPGRADE A BURGER. YOU'LL FEEL LIKE A BOSS.

LOADED TANDOORI FRIES

THIS IS LATE-NIGHT FOOD WITH MAIN CHARACTER ENERGY. AIR-FRIED CHIPS BURIED UNDER JUICY TANDOORI CHICKEN, MELTY CHEESE, AND FRESH TOPPINGS. EAT IT FROM THE TRAY. NO SHAME.

YOU'LL NEED:
2 SKIN-ON CHICKEN THIGHS OR 1 BREAST, CHOPPED
1 TSP TANDOORI SPICE MIX
1 TBSP YOGHURT (ANY KIND WILL DO)
FROZEN FRIES (AS MUCH AS YOUR HUNGER DEMANDS)
HANDFUL OF GRATED CHEESE
RED ONION, THINLY SLICED
FRESH CORIANDER OR PARSLEY (OPTIONAL, BUT CLASSY)
DRIZZLE OF GARLIC MAYO OR CHILLI SAUCE
METHOD:
MIX THE CHICKEN WITH YOGHURT AND TANDOORI SPICE. LET IT SIT WHILE YOU SORT THE CHIPS.
AIR-FRY THE FROZEN FRIES AT 200°C FOR 12-15 MINUTES, SHAKING HALFWAY UNTIL GOLDEN AND CRISP.
THROW THE CHICKEN INTO THE AIR FRYER AND COOK AT 190°C FOR 10-12 MINUTES UNTIL COOKED THROUGH AND SLIGHTLY CHARRED.
PILE THE CHIPS ONTO A TRAY OR PLATE, LOAD UP WITH THE CHICKEN, SPRINKLE CHEESE ON TOP, THEN BLAST IT ALL FOR ANOTHER 2-3 MINS TO MELT.
TOP WITH RED ONION, HERBS IF YOU'RE FEELING POSH, AND DRIZZLE OVER GARLIC MAYO OR CHILLI SAUCE LIKE YOU'RE PAINTING A MASTERPIECE.

LAD TIP: ADD A SQUIRT OF LEMON OR LIME ON TOP BEFORE SERVING. MAKES IT FEEL FRESH... EVEN IF YOU'RE EATING IT IN YOUR BOXERS AT 1AM.

BUFFALO CAULI BITES

Hear me out. These little cauliflower bites are spicy, crispy, and covered in buffalo sauce so good it should be illegal. You won't miss the meat – not because you've gone soft, but because this stuff just works.

You'll need:
Half a head of cauliflower, chopped into bite-sized chunks
2 tbsp plain flour
2 tbsp milk
1 tsp garlic powder
Pinch of salt
Bit of oil spray
For the sauce:
2 tbsp hot sauce (Frank's RedHot is king)
1 tbsp melted butter
1 tsp honey

Method:
Whisk the flour, milk, garlic powder, and salt into a thick batter.
Dip the cauliflower chunks in the batter and let the excess drip off.
Air fry at 200°C for 12–15 minutes, shaking halfway until crispy and golden.
While they're cooking, mix up the buffalo sauce. Heat the hot sauce, butter, and honey in a small pan or microwave – just enough to blend.
When the cauli bites are done, toss them in the sauce or drizzle it over like a boss. Serve hot and smug.

Lad Tip: Add a pot of blue cheese dip on the side. Not essential – just elite.

HEATING ELEMENT

CHAPTER THREE: PROPER STODGE

FAN

HOT AIR BLAST

CRISPER BASKET

DIRTY DONER WRAPS

This one tastes like a 2am takeaway but costs less than a pint and doesn't come with regret. Juicy, spiced meat cooked right in your air fryer, stuffed into wraps with all the gear. You won't believe you made it yourself.

You'll need:
250g lamb mince (or beef if you prefer)
1 tsp cumin
1 tsp paprika
1 tsp garlic powder
1 tsp mixed herbs
Salt and pepper
2 tortilla wraps
Shredded lettuce, sliced red onion, chilli sauce, garlic mayo – the full works

Method:
Mix the mince with all the spices and a pinch of salt and pepper. Shape it into a tight loaf shape with your hands – about the size of a chunky sausage roll.
Air fry at 180°C for 15–18 minutes, turning halfway, until cooked through with a little crispy edge. Let it rest for a minute before slicing thin.
Warm the wraps for 1 minute in the air fryer or microwave.
Load them up with meat, lettuce, onion, and sauces. Wrap it tight, eat it fast, and prepare for greatness.

Lad Tip: Double the mix, slice the meat up, and freeze the extra – future you will thank you on a hangover.

CHEESE-STUFFED BURGERS

Juicy on the outside, molten cheese on the inside. These burgers are pure filth in the best way. Smash it in a bun, add your toppings, and you'll never go back to plain patties again.

You'll need:
250g beef mince
Salt, pepper, garlic granules
2 thick slices of cheddar or mozzarella
Burger buns
Lettuce, tomato, gherkins, burger sauce – all the good stuff

Method:
Season your mince with salt, pepper, and garlic granules.
Split it into two balls. Flatten each into a wide, thin patty.
Place a slice of cheese in the centre of one patty, then cover it with the second one. Seal the edges tight so no cheese escapes (or at least try).
Air fry at 200°C for 10–12 minutes, flipping halfway.
Toast your buns in the air fryer for the last 2 minutes.
Build it how you like it – lettuce, sauce, pickles, a little burger swagger.

Lad Tip: Feeling spicy? Add a dollop of jalapeño relish inside with the cheese. You'll need a cold drink after, but it's worth it.

BBQ CHICKEN & WAFFLE STACK

This is proper American-style comfort food – crispy chicken bites stacked on golden waffles, dripping in BBQ sauce. It's sweet, savoury, and scandalous. Fork and knife optional. Shame? None.

You'll need:
2 chicken thighs, chopped
1 tsp smoked paprika
1 tsp garlic powder
Pinch of salt and pepper
2 frozen waffles
2 tbsp BBQ sauce
Bit of oil spray

Method:
Toss the chopped chicken in smoked paprika, garlic powder, salt, and pepper.
Air fry at 200°C for 12-15 minutes until golden, crispy, and cooked through.
While that's cooking, warm your waffles – either in the toaster or air fryer for 3-4 mins.
In the last 2 minutes of cooking, pour BBQ sauce over the chicken in the fryer basket so it gets sticky and caramelised.
Stack it: waffle, BBQ chicken, waffle, more chicken, drizzle of extra sauce.
You're now legally married to your dinner.

Lad Tip: Add a drizzle of maple syrup if you're feeling bold. It sounds mad. It tastes unreal.

MEGA MAC & CHEESE BALLS

Leftover mac and cheese? Turn it into crispy golden snack bombs that ooze when you bite. These bad lads are dangerous – make a few, and you'll wish you made twenty.

You'll need:
1 bowl of leftover mac & cheese (cold – fridge cold works best)
1 egg
Breadcrumbs (panko if you're fancy)
Bit of flour
Bit of oil spray
Pinch of black pepper

Method:
Scoop out handfuls of mac & cheese and roll into tight balls – ping pong size. If it's too sloppy, mix in a spoonful of flour.
Set up a dunk station: one bowl of flour, one beaten egg, one bowl of breadcrumbs.
Roll each ball through flour, egg, then crumbs. Coat well.
Chill the balls in the fridge for 10–15 mins if you can – helps keep 'em together.
Air fry at 200°C for 8–10 minutes, spray with oil, and flip halfway. You're looking for golden and crispy.

Lad Tip: Serve with hot sauce, ranch, or just shovel 'em in solo. No one's judging.

CHICKEN KIEV JACKET POTATOES

Proper British stodge with a cheeky twist. Fluffy spuds stuffed with garlicky chicken and a pool of buttery sauce that soaks into every bite. It's a jacket with attitude.

You'll need:
2 medium baking potatoes
1 chicken breast, chopped
1 tsp garlic granules
1 tbsp butter
Pinch of parsley (fresh or dried)
Salt and pepper
Grated cheese (optional but not really)

Method:
Stab your potatoes a few times with a fork, rub with a bit of oil and salt, and air fry at 200°C for 35-45 minutes until crispy on the outside and fluffy inside. While they're cooking, season the chicken with salt, pepper, and garlic granules.
Air fry the chicken at 180°C for 10-12 minutes, flipping halfway.
Melt the butter and stir in some parsley and extra garlic if you fancy.
Once the potatoes are done, cut them open like you mean it. Fluff the insides with a fork, then stuff in the chopped chicken and pour over that garlic butter like you're painting a masterpiece.
Top with cheese if you're going full beast mode and give it another 2-3 minutes to melt.

Lad Tip: Got any peas or sweetcorn lying about? Mix 'em in the filling to feel like you've eaten a vegetable today.

CHAPTER FOUR:
15-MINUTE FIXES

GARLIC PARMESAN CHIPS

These ain't your soggy oven fries. We're talking crispy golden chips coated in garlic butter and dusted in Parmesan like they're ready for a night out. Simple, fast, dangerously addictive.

You'll need:
Frozen chips or homemade (thin-cut works best)
1 tbsp butter
1 tsp garlic powder
Grated Parmesan (the stuff in a tub or fresh – up to you)
Salt and pepper
Bit of oil spray

Method:
Air fry the chips at 200°C for 12-15 minutes, shake halfway. You want 'em golden and crispy – no half-jobs.
While that's going, melt the butter and stir in garlic powder, a pinch of salt, and a crack of black pepper.
Once the chips are done, chuck them in a bowl and pour over the garlic butter. Toss them around, then hit them with a snowstorm of Parmesan.
Serve hot, loud, and proud.

Lad Tip: Add chopped parsley or chilli flakes if you're feeling gourmet. Or don't. They'll still bang either way.

40

MOZZARELLA PIZZA SWIRLS

Cheesy, saucy, flaky spirals of pizza joy. These little rolls are crispy on the outside, gooey in the middle, and gone in about 30 seconds flat. Perfect for mates, movie nights, or just not sharing at all.

You'll need:
1 sheet of ready-rolled puff pastry (from the fridge section)
2 tbsp pizza sauce or passata
Handful of grated mozzarella
Pinch of oregano or mixed herbs
Bit of oil spray or egg wash

Method:
Unroll the puff pastry and spread a thin layer of pizza sauce all over it. Don't drown it.
Sprinkle mozzarella across the top and a pinch of herbs.
Roll it up lengthways into a long tube, then slice into 1-inch thick swirls.
Lay them flat in the air fryer basket. Spray lightly with oil or brush with egg wash if you're fancy.
Air fry at 190°C for 8-10 minutes until golden, puffed, and oozing cheese.

Lad Tip: Want pepperoni in the mix? Lay some slices down before you roll it. Instant upgrade.

CRISPY FISH FINGER TACOS

Fish fingers in a taco? You bet. Crunchy, saucy, and ridiculously easy. It's comfort food with a glow-up – cheap to make, big on taste, and zero cutlery required.

You'll need:
4 fish fingers (the good ones or whatever's on offer)
2 small soft tortillas
Handful of shredded lettuce or slaw
Tartare sauce or mayo
Lemon wedge
Optional: pickled onions, hot sauce, or jalapeños if you're feeling spicy

Method:
Air fry the fish fingers at 200°C for 10–12 minutes until golden and crispy.
Warm the tortillas in the air fryer or microwave – just a minute will do.
Layer lettuce (or slaw) on each wrap, drop two fish fingers on top, then hit it with tartare sauce and a squeeze of lemon.
Add extras like hot sauce, pickles, or jalapeños if you're about that bold life.
Fold, bite, and wonder why you ever ate fish fingers with oven chips like a child.

Lad Tip: Double up the fish fingers per taco if you're hungry. You're not six years old anymore.

SALT & PEPPER CHICKEN

A proper fakeaway legend. Crispy chicken, tossed in spicy salt and pepper seasoning with peppers and onions for that classic crunch. It's loud, it's bold, and it tastes like a win.

You'll need:
2 chicken thighs or 1 large breast, chopped into chunks
2 tbsp cornflour
1 tsp Chinese five spice
Half a red pepper, sliced
Half an onion, sliced
1 chilli, sliced (optional but recommended)
2 spring onions, chopped
Salt and white pepper
Bit of oil spray

Method:
Toss the chicken in cornflour, five spice, a pinch of salt and white pepper. Get it coated.
Air fry at 200°C for 12-14 minutes, flipping halfway. It should be golden and crispy.
While that's going, chuck the peppers, onions, and chilli into the air fryer or fry in a pan for 4-5 minutes until softened with a bit of char.
Mix the cooked chicken and veg together, sprinkle in extra salt, white pepper, and spring onions. Toss it all like you're working the wok at your local.
Serve hot, with rice, noodles, or straight out the bowl like a kitchen goblin.

Lad Tip: Double the batch and reheat leftovers for the best lunch of your life. Or just eat the lot now. We don't judge.

THAI SWEET CHILLI NOODLE BOX

Sticky, spicy, saucy noodles that hit every craving at once. Toss in whatever veg or meat you've got – this one's built for lazy brilliance. It's fast, flexible, and full of kick.

You'll need:
1 pack of pre-cooked noodles (straight-to-wok style)
1 tbsp sweet chilli sauce
1 tsp soy sauce
1 tsp sesame oil (optional but next level)
Half a pepper, sliced
Handful of shredded carrot or cabbage
1 egg (optional – for scrambling)
Chilli flakes or sriracha if you want heat
Method:
Throw your veg in the air fryer at 200°C for 4–5 mins with a quick spray of oil. Just enough to soften with a bit of edge.
While that's cooking, mix your noodles with sweet chilli sauce, soy, and sesame oil.
Add everything to a heatproof dish (like foil or a little tin tray). Crack an egg in there if you're going full stir-fry mode.
Air fry at 180°C for 5–7 minutes. Stir halfway so the sauce coats every strand and the egg scrambles into the mix.
Serve in a bowl, eat with a fork or chopsticks, and don't talk to anyone until it's gone.

Lad Tip: Throw in cooked chicken, prawns, or tofu if you're on a protein buzz. Or just pile it high and call it dinner.

CHAPTER FIVE: DATE NIGHT DINNERS

19. HONEY GARLIC SALMON
20. HERBY CHICKEN PARCELS
21. LOADED STEAK & PEPPER FLATBREAD
22. FETA & SPINACH-STUFFED MUSHROOMS

HONEY GARLIC SALMON

This one's smooth, sweet, and suspiciously grown-up. Flaky salmon coated in a sticky glaze, done in under 15, and guaranteed to make you look like you know what you're doing. Serve it up with rice, noodles, or something green if you're faking health.

You'll need:
2 salmon fillets
1 tbsp honey
1 tbsp soy sauce
1 tsp garlic (paste or finely chopped)
1 tsp oil
Pinch of chilli flakes (optional – for heat)
Lemon wedge, for vibes
Method:
Mix the honey, soy, garlic, oil, and chilli flakes into a glaze. Taste it. If it slaps, you're good.
Brush the glaze over the salmon fillets. Let them sit for 5-10 minutes if you've got time.
Air fry at 180°C for 10–12 minutes, skin-side down, until golden and flaky.
Serve with rice, noodles, or buttery greens. Add the lemon wedge like a pro.
Eat like you're in a bistro. Ignore the fact you're in socks and trackies.

Lad Tip: Do the washing up before she gets there. Trust me – nothing ruins a vibe like crusty forks in the sink.

HERBY CHICKEN PARCELS

Moist chicken, wrapped in puff pastry with herbs, garlic, and cheesy goodness inside. It's like a roast dinner's fancy cousin who just got back from Europe. Crispy outside, juicy inside – and dead easy to smash out.

You'll need:
1 sheet of ready-rolled puff pastry
2 small chicken breasts or fillets
1 tsp mixed herbs
1 garlic clove, crushed (or paste)
1 tbsp cream cheese or grated cheddar
Bit of oil or egg wash
Salt and pepper

Method:
Preheat air fryer to 190°C.
Flatten the chicken slightly with your hand. Rub with garlic, herbs, salt and pepper.
Cut the pastry in half and place a chicken fillet on each half. Add a spoon of cream cheese or a pinch of grated cheddar on top.
Fold the pastry over like a parcel, seal the edges with a fork, and give the tops a brush of oil or egg wash for that golden glow-up.
Air fry for 15–18 minutes until the pastry's crisp and puffed and the chicken's cooked through.
Slice it open and pretend you've been watching cooking shows instead of football clips.

Lad Tip: Serve with roast veg, mash, or just a heap of chips. Either way, it looks fancy. Tastes even fancier.

LOADED STEAK & PEPPER FLATBREAD

Tender steak, sweet peppers, melty cheese – all slammed into a warm flatbread. It's got that street food energy with steakhouse flavour, and it's all done in one fryer tray. Absolute scenes.

You'll need:
1 flat iron steak or rump (150–200g)
Half a red pepper, sliced
Half a red onion, sliced
Handful of grated mozzarella or cheddar
1 flatbread or naan
Olive oil
Salt, pepper, garlic powder
Drizzle of chilli sauce or garlic mayo (optional but yes)

Method:
Rub the steak with a little oil, salt, pepper, and garlic powder. Let it chill while you cook the veg.
Air fry the peppers and onions at 200°C for 6–8 minutes until soft and slightly charred.
Chuck the steak in the air fryer – 190°C for 6–8 minutes depending on how you like it. Rest it for a few minutes, then slice it thin.
Warm your flatbread for a minute in the fryer, then load it up: steak, veg, cheese, sauce.
Fold it, roll it, or eat it like a pizza. Either way, it's pure flavour.
Lad Tip: Add jalapeños or crispy onions for extra kick. Or keep it classic and let the steak speak for itself.

FETA & SPINACH-STUFFED MUSHROOMS

Big, juicy mushrooms loaded with creamy spinach, salty feta, and baked to crispy-topped perfection. It's the kind of dish that says "I read cookbooks" when really you just know how to use an air fryer like a boss.

You'll need:
2 large portobello mushrooms
1 handful of fresh spinach (or frozen, defrosted and squeezed dry)
50g feta cheese
1 garlic clove (crushed)
1 tbsp cream cheese
Bit of oil
Salt and pepper
Breadcrumbs (optional for crunch)

Method:
Wipe the mushrooms clean and remove the stalks.
In a pan or microwave, wilt the spinach and mix it with the garlic, cream cheese, crumbled feta, and a pinch of salt and pepper.
Stuff the mix into the mushroom caps. Top with a sprinkle of breadcrumbs if you want a bit of crunch.
Drizzle with oil and air fry at 180°C for 10–12 minutes until the mushrooms are cooked through and the tops are golden and bubbling.

Lad Tip: Serve with garlic bread or a side salad if you're trying to look balanced. Or just eat both mushrooms and call it a meal.

INSIDE AN AIR FRYER

HEATING
ELEMENT

CHAPTER SIX:
LATE NIGHT
CRAVINGS

FAN

HOT AIR
BLASTER

CRISPER
BASKET

CHILLI CHEESE NACHO BITES

Crunchy on the outside, molten cheese and spicy kick on the inside. These little flavour bombs are the ultimate snack attack – perfect for solo sofa sessions or impressing your mates during match day.

You'll need:
1 handful of crushed nachos or tortilla chips
100g cream cheese
50g grated cheddar
1 tsp chopped jalapeños
1 spring onion, chopped
Pinch of paprika
1 egg
Breadcrumbs
Bit of oil spray

Method:
Mix the cream cheese, cheddar, jalapeños, spring onion, and paprika into one glorious spicy mess.
Scoop out little chunks and roll into balls. Stick them in the freezer for 10 minutes to firm up.
Dip each ball in beaten egg, then roll through crushed nachos or breadcrumbs until fully coated.
Air fry at 200°C for 6–8 minutes, flipping halfway, until golden and crispy.
Serve hot and molten. You'll burn your mouth. You won't care.

Lad Tip: Got some sour cream or salsa lying about? Use it. These were made for dipping.

STICKY BBQ RIBS

These ribs are fall-apart tender with a sweet, smoky glaze that clings to your fingers like a good night out. You don't need a smoker or a grill – the air fryer does all the heavy lifting.

You'll need:
Half a rack of pork ribs (pre-cooked or parboiled if you're short on time)
3 tbsp BBQ sauce
1 tsp honey
1 tsp smoked paprika
Splash of vinegar (malt or apple cider – whatever's handy)
Salt and pepper

Method:
If your ribs are raw, boil them first for 20-25 mins to soften them up. If they're pre-cooked, you're golden.
Mix your BBQ sauce, honey, paprika, vinegar, and a bit of salt and pepper into a glaze.
Coat the ribs in the sauce, making sure they're fully covered. Get your hands messy – it's the law.
Air fry at 180°C for 10-15 minutes, flipping once, until the sauce caramelises and the edges get a bit crisp and charred.
Let them rest for a couple of minutes (if you can wait). Then tear in like a caveman.

Lad Tip: Want 'em even saucier? Save a bit of glaze and brush it on halfway through cooking. Extra messy, extra good.

LOADED CURLY FRIES

Golden curly fries buried under melted cheese, crispy bacon, and whatever else you fancy chucking on. This isn't just a snack – it's a full-blown event. Grab a fork or dive in bare-handed. We won't tell.

You'll need:
Frozen curly fries (obviously)
2 rashers of bacon, chopped
Handful of grated cheddar or mozzarella
2 spring onions, sliced
Sour cream or burger sauce (optional but highly encouraged)
Jalapeños or hot sauce if you're living dangerously

Method:
Air fry your curly fries at 200°C for 12–15 minutes until golden and crispy.
Chuck the bacon in the fryer for the last 5–6 minutes or do it in a pan – just get it crispy.
Once the fries are done, load them up in a tray: fries first, then bacon, then cheese.
Air fry again for 2–3 minutes to melt the cheese and bring the chaos together.
Top with spring onions, sour cream, and anything else you've got in the fridge that makes you feel like a legend.

Lad Tip: Use leftover chilli or pulled pork on top and call it "gourmet." No one needs to know it came from Tuesday's dinner.

DEEP-FRIED OREOS

Crispy on the outside, soft and warm in the middle – these little dessert bombs are dangerously good. Dunked in batter, air-fried to golden perfection, and gone in seconds. You've been warned.

You'll need:
6 Oreos
4 tbsp plain flour
2 tbsp milk
1 tsp sugar
1 tsp vanilla extract (optional)
1/2 tsp baking powder
Bit of oil spray
Icing sugar (for dusting)

Method:
Mix the flour, milk, sugar, baking powder, and vanilla (if using) into a thick pancake-like batter.
Dip each Oreo in the batter until it's fully coated – no gaps.
Place them in the air fryer basket, spray with a bit of oil, and cook at 180°C for 6-8 minutes until golden and puffed.
Dust with icing sugar like a boss and eat while warm.

Lad Tip: Got some ice cream in the freezer? Serve these on top and make your kitchen look like a dessert bar. Boom.

COOKIE DOUGH CROISSANTS

Shop-bought croissant dough stuffed with chocolate chip cookie dough and air-fried to golden, gooey perfection. This isn't just dessert. This is edible therapy. Comfort in pastry form.

You'll need:
1 tube of ready-to-roll croissant dough (or a few frozen ones, defrosted)
6 tsp cookie dough (ready-made or homemade – no judgment)
Bit of oil spray or melted butter
Icing sugar or melted chocolate (if you want to flex)

Method:
Unroll the croissant dough and separate into triangles.
Drop a teaspoon of cookie dough onto the wide end of each triangle.
Roll it up tight like a normal croissant – make sure the dough seals the filling inside.
Brush with melted butter or give a light spray of oil.
Air fry at 180°C for 8-10 minutes until puffed, golden, and just starting to ooze.
Dust with icing sugar or drizzle with melted chocolate if you want to act like a dessert king.

Lad Tip: These are even better dipped in cold milk or eaten while watching something you'll never admit to enjoying. Bliss.

HEATING
ELEMENT

CHAPTER SEVEN: BULK MEALS FOR BROKE DAYS

28. AIR-FRIED PASTA BAKE
29. DIRTY RICE WITH CHICKEN & VEG
30. SPICY SAUSAGE TRAYBAKE

CRISPER
BASKET

AIR-FRIED PASTA BAKE

Cheap. Cheesy. Chuck-it-all-in greatness. This pasta bake is perfect for leftovers, meal prep, or feeding yourself for three days off one tray. You'll feel rich even if your bank balance says otherwise.

You'll need:
200g dried pasta (penne, fusilli – whatever's in the cupboard)
1 cup pasta sauce (tomato, arrabbiata, or anything red and ready)
100g grated cheese (cheddar, mozzarella, or a mix)
Optional: cooked sausage, bacon, chicken, or frozen veg
Salt, pepper, dried herbs
Bit of oil spray

Method:
Boil the pasta until just cooked, drain, and toss with a little oil so it doesn't stick.
Mix the pasta with sauce, half the cheese, and whatever extras you're throwing in.
Season with salt, pepper, and a pinch of herbs.
Pour it all into a foil tray or oven-safe dish that fits in your air fryer.
Top with the rest of the cheese and air fry at 180°C for 10–12 minutes until the top's golden and bubbling like lava.
Let it cool slightly so you don't scorch your tongue. Or don't. Live dangerously.

Lad Tip: Make it in bulk, stick portions in the fridge, and reheat in the air fryer when hunger strikes. Meal prep, lad-style.

DIRTY RICE WITH CHICKEN & VEG

Rice, spice, meat, and whatever veg is clinging on in your fridge. It's smoky, hearty, and tastes like it took hours — but it's done in 20. The kind of meal that slaps harder the next day.

You'll need:
1 cup cooked rice (day-old is best, fresh works too)
1 chicken thigh or breast, chopped
Half a pepper, diced
1 small onion, chopped
Handful of frozen peas or sweetcorn
1 tsp smoked paprika
1 tsp garlic powder
Pinch of chilli flakes (optional)
Salt and pepper
Bit of oil spray

Method:
Air fry the chicken at 200°C for 10-12 minutes with paprika, garlic powder, salt and pepper. Flip halfway so it gets that char.
Chuck in the veg during the last 5 minutes so it softens and soaks up flavour.
Mix the cooked rice into the tray with the chicken and veg. Add a touch more seasoning and a splash of oil if it's looking dry.
Air fry for another 4-5 minutes to heat through and crisp the edges slightly.
Serve it hot. Eat it straight from the tray if no one's watching. Or even if they are.

Lad Tip: Add a fried egg on top and call it deluxe. You'll feel like a street food chef with zero training.

SPICY SAUSAGE TRAYBAKE

This is the one-tray wonder. Spicy sausages, crispy potatoes, charred veg – all roasted together in one glorious, greasy masterpiece. It's cheap, tasty, and clears half your fridge in the process.

You'll need:
4 sausages (spicy ones if you're bold, plain if you're soft)
2 medium potatoes, chopped into chunks
1 red onion, sliced
1 pepper, chopped
1 tsp paprika
1 tsp garlic granules
1 tbsp oil
Salt and pepper
Optional: drizzle of hot sauce or mustard at the end

Method:
Chuck all the veg and potatoes into a mixing bowl with oil, paprika, garlic granules, salt and pepper. Toss it so everything's coated.
Lay it all in a foil tray or straight into the air fryer tray if it's big enough. Nestle the sausages in on top.
Air fry at 190°C for 20–25 minutes, shaking halfway. Sausages should be golden, potatoes crispy, veg slightly charred.
Plate it up (or eat from the tray like a champion), and finish with a drizzle of sauce if you fancy.

Lad Tip: Leftovers? Chop 'em up the next morning and fry with an egg. That's hangover-proof magic.

The Hangover Recovery Air Fry Menu

If your head's pounding and your fridge looks bleak... fire up salvation, lad. These are the ultimate air-fried cures for a night that got out of hand:

- Hashbrown Stack: Layer hashbrowns, cheese, and sausage. Air fry until golden.
- Cheesy Sausage Wraps: Wrap cooked sausages in tortillas with cheese. 5 mins in the fryer.
- Bacon-Crisp Butty: Air fry bacon to a crunch, throw in a soft roll, and drown in ketchup. – Garlic Revival Toast: Bread + butter + garlic powder + cheese = magic.
- Full English (Air-Fried): Sausage, mushrooms, beans (in foil), and a fried egg finale.

78

Top 10 Lad-Level Air Fryer Hacks

1. Add a splash of water to the drawer for crispier chips and less smoke.

2. Wrap bacon in foil - zero cleanup, full flavour.

3. No need to preheat - just add 2 extra minutes to your timer.

4. Use baking paper for sticky stuff like BBQ wings.

5. Reheat pizza in the air fryer - it'll taste better than fresh.

6. Toast your sarnies with a slice of cheese on top.

7. Line the drawer with foil shaped like a tray for saucy meals.

8. Air fry your garlic bread for a crunchy edge and soft middle.

9. Toss frozen chips with a little oil and seasoning before cooking. 10. Use an upside-down ramekin to cook steak evenly on both sides.

Build Your Own Mega-Mix Tray
The 'Tray of Destiny'. One tray. All the power. Mix and match for a feast of champions: Base: Chips / Wedges / Curly Fries
Protein: Chicken Nuggets / Sausages / Kebab Meat
Topper: Cheese / Jalapenos / Fried Onions
Drizzle: BBQ Sauce / Mayo / Sriracha

YOU'VE DONE IT, MATE.

YOU'VE COOKED YOUR WAY THROUGH BREAKFASTS, BURGERS, FAKEAWAYS, AND LATE-NIGHT CRAVINGS. YOU'VE SMASHED CHEESY MELTS, MADE YOUR OWN DONER, AND TURNED HALF A FRIDGE OF SCRAPS INTO DINNER LIKE SOME KIND OF KITCHEN WIZARD.

AND YOU DID IT ALL WITH ONE AIR FRYER AND ABOUT 30 MINUTES OF EFFORT. THAT'S LEGENDARY BEHAVIOUR.

THIS BOOK WASN'T ABOUT BEING PERFECT. IT WAS ABOUT GETTING FED, GETTING FLAVOUR, AND GETTING YOUR CONFIDENCE UP BEHIND A FRYER THAT'S SMARTER THAN HALF THE BLOKES ON TELLY. YOU'VE PROVED YOU DON'T NEED FANCY GEAR, POSH INGREDIENTS, OR A MICHELIN STAR – JUST A BIT OF HEAT, A BIT OF HUNGER, AND A DECENT PLAYLIST IN THE BACKGROUND.

SO KEEP COOKING. TRY YOUR OWN TWISTS. SHARE IT WITH YOUR MATES. OR DON'T. KEEP THE GOOD STUFF TO YOURSELF.

AND REMEMBER – IF ALL ELSE FAILS: CHUCK IT IN, TURN IT UP, AND TRUST THE AIR FRYER.

STAY CRISPY, STAY FULL, AND STAY CLASS.

– FROM ONE HUNGRY LAD TO ANOTHER.

Printed in Dunstable, United Kingdom

75408396R00047